T0012198

SIGHT READING
& RHYTHM
EVERY DAY®

Helen Marlais with Kevin Olson

THE
F·J·H
MUSIC
COMPANY
INC.
Frank J. Hackinson

Production: Frank J. Hackinson
Production Coordinators: Philip Groeber and Isabel Otero Bowen
Cover: Terpstra Design, San Francisco
Text Design and Layout: Terpstra Design and Maritza Cosano Gomez
Engraving: Kevin Olson and Tempo Music Press, Inc.
Printer: Tempo Music Press, Inc.

ISBN-13: 978-1-56939-501-1

ABOUT THE AUTHORS

Helen Marlais' active performance schedule includes concerts in North America, Western and Eastern Europe, the Middle East, and Asia, and her travels abroad have included performing and teaching at the leading conservatories in Lithuania, Estonia, Italy, France, Hungary, Turkey, Russia, China, and England. She has performed with members of the Pittsburgh, Minnesota, Grand Rapids, Des Moines, Cedar Rapids, and Beijing National Symphony Orchestras to name a few, and is recorded on Stargrass Records®, Gasparo, and Centaur record labels. She has had numerous collaborative performances broadcast regionally, nationally, and internationally on radio, television, and the Internet with her husband, clarinetist Arthur Campbell. She presents workshops at every national convention and is a featured presenter at state conventions. She has been a guest teacher and performer at leading music schools and conservatories throughout North America, Europe, and Asia. Dr. Marlais is the Director of Keyboard Publications for The FJH Music Company Inc. Her articles can be read in *Keyboard Companion, The American Music Teacher,* and *Clavier* magazines.

Dr. Marlais is an associate professor of piano at Grand Valley State University in Grand Rapids, Michigan, where she directs the piano pedagogy program, coordinates the group piano programs, and teaches studio piano. She received her DM in piano performance and pedagogy from Northwestern University and her MM in piano performance from Carnegie Mellon University. She has also held full-time faculty piano positions at the Crane School of Music, S.U.N.Y. at Potsdam, Iowa State University, and Gustavus Adolphus College. Visit: www.helenmarlais.com.

Kevin Olson is an active pianist, composer, and faculty member at Elmhurst College near Chicago, Illinois, where he teaches classical and jazz piano, music theory, and electronic music. He holds a Doctor of Education degree from National-Louis University, and bachelor's and master's degrees in music composition and theory from Brigham Young University. Before teaching at Elmhurst College, he held a visiting professor position at Humboldt State University in California.

A native of Utah, Kevin began composing at the age of five. When he was twelve, his composition *An American Trainride* received the Overall First Prize at the 1983 National PTA Convention in Albuquerque, New Mexico. Since then, he has been a composer-in- residence at the National Conference on Piano Pedagogy and has written music for the American Piano Quartet, Chicago a cappella, the Rich Matteson Jazz Festival, and several piano teachers associations around the country.

Kevin maintains a large piano studio, teaching students of a variety of ages and abilities. Many of the needs of his own piano students have inspired a diverse collection of books and solos published by The FJH Music Company Inc., which he joined as a writer in 1994.

HOW THE SERIES IS ORGANIZED

All rhythmic activities

All sight-reading activities

Place a ✔ when you have been successful!

Each unit of the series is divided into five separate days of enjoyable rhythmic and sight-reading activities. Students complete these short activities "Every Day" at home, by themselves. Every day the words, "Did It!" are found in a box for the student to check once they have completed both the rhythm and sight-reading activities.

The new concepts are identified in the upper right-hand corner of each unit. Once introduced, these concepts are continually reinforced through subsequent units.

On the lesson day, there are short rhythmic and sight-reading activities that will take only minutes for the teacher and student to do together. An enjoyable sight-reading duet wraps up each unit.

BOOKS 2A AND 2B

Rhythm:

Eighth notes are introduced in book 2A, and eighth note rests as well as upbeats (pick-ups) are introduced in book 2B.

Rhythmic activities in books 2A/B include the following:

- Students are asked to count rhythmic examples out loud and clap, tap, point, snap their fingers, and march.

- Students learn directional reading.

- Students speak lyrics in rhythm.

- Students add bar lines and missing beats to excerpts and then count the rhythmic examples out loud.

- Students are asked to pulse with their feet and march in step, to feel a constant pulse.

- Students are asked to clap rhythmic examples by memory, an excellent ear training and memory exercise.

- Students tap different rhythms in both hands.

- Students learn and drill $\frac{2}{4}$, $\frac{3}{4}$, $\frac{4}{4}$, and $\frac{6}{4}$ time signatures.

Fingering:

Very little fingering is provided so that students learn how to plan their fingering when sight reading.

Reading:

Students start book 2A with a general review of intervals (2nds through 5ths), and a review of C, G, and F major. Then, students sight read melodies in the following keys: G, D, A, and E major, and A, D, E, C, G, and F minor. Five-finger patterns are reinforced as well as single-line music played *between* the hands.

Harmonic and melodic intervals, as well as phrasing are continuously reinforced. Students sight read and transpose musical examples as well.

In book 2B, students learn triads and begin to play pieces with both hands together on two staffs. Pieces using tonic triads are introduced as well as parallel-motion melodies for both hands. Attention is given to different articulations and dynamics, and students are asked to transpose short pieces to the next nearest key.

Sight Reading activities include the following:

- The student learns to "plan" for note and rhythmic accuracy, correct articulations, and a good sound.

- Helpful suggestions guide students to think before they play, and not stop once they have started!

- Students are asked to silently play melodies or tap the rhythm before playing some of the excerpts, which encourages them to maintain a constant pulse and the forward motion of the musical line.

- Students circle and analyze intervals and patterns before playing.

- The metronome is incorporated often.

Developing these important skills lays the proper foundation for music making and fosters stellar piano playing. A student who sight reads well has the skills to progress rapidly and enjoy success. *Sight Reading & Rhythm Every Day®* is a sure way to produce the positive results that motivate students.

TABLE OF CONTENTS

Unit 1   New Concept: eighth notes. Review of intervals
(2nds through 5ths) and melodies starting on middle C 6

Unit 2   Review of intervals (2nds through 5ths); melodies starting on treble G
and bass F; $\frac{3}{4}$ time signature; *legato* and *staccato* articulations 10

Unit 3   Review of intervals (2nds through 5ths); melodies starting on treble C
and bass C; $\frac{2}{4}$ time signature 14

Unit 4   New Concepts: major five-finger patterns: G, D, A, and E;
$\frac{6}{4}$ time signature 18

Unit 5   New Concept: minor five-finger patterns: A, D, and E 22

Unit 6   New Concept: minor five-finger patterns: C, G, and F 26

Unit 7   New Concept: melodies played *between* the hands in C, G, and
F major using seconds, thirds, fourths, and fifths 30

Unit 8   New Concept: melodies played *between* the hands in D, A, and
E major using seconds, thirds, fourths, and fifths 34

Unit 9   New Concept: transposition from C to D major and F to G major.
Review of single-line music played *between* the hands 38

Unit 10   Review of all concepts 42

          Additional Sight Reading Exercises 48

Unit 1

New Concept: eighth notes.

Review of intervals (2nds through 5ths);
melodies starting on middle C

 Rhythm—Clap the following rhythmic examples and count with energy!

DID IT!

Place a ✔ when you have been successful!

Sight reading—Tap and count the rhythm before playing.
Circle the repeated notes before you begin to play.

Rhythm—Point to each note as you count along.
Whisper the beats during rests.

DID IT!

Sight reading—Count the rhythm of these melodies silently while following the music with your
eyes. Then play without stopping!

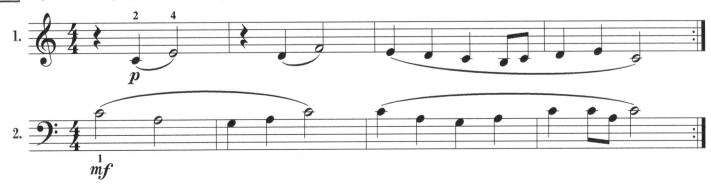

FJH15

Rhythm—Speak the lyrics in rhythm while you point to each note.

DID IT!

1. I love cher-ry pie topped with ice cream with a ti-ny lit-tle cher-ry on top!

2. Hey, Mis-ter Chip-munk, why do you stare at me? Do you want a lit-tle bit of my lunch?

Sight reading—Tap the rhythm before playing.
Play and sing the melody, and don't stop once you have started!

DAY FOUR

Rhythm—Add bar lines to the following rhythms.
When you have finished, clap and count each line twice.

DID IT!

Sight reading—Study the rhythm and direction of the moving notes below.
Block all of the melodic fifths (play together) before playing. Then play as written.

Rhythm—Fill in the missing beats of the following measures with either a note or a rest so that each adds up to $\frac{4}{4}$ time. Then clap and count.

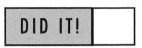

1.

2.

 Sight reading—With the metronome set at ♩ = 80, clap or tap the following examples. Then play these at the same metronome speed. Always look ahead!

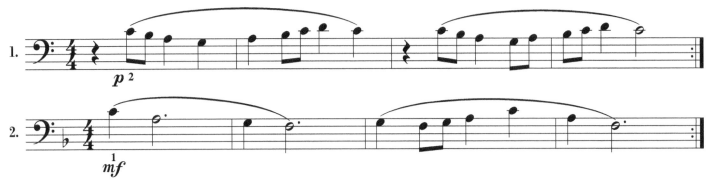

1.

2.

 ★ LESSON DAY

 Rhythm—Clap and count out loud the following examples for your teacher. First clap each one slowly, then both quickly. You can decide with your teacher if the examples were steady at both tempos!

1.

2.

Sight reading—Your teacher will play one of the following melodies. Point to the melody that you hear. Then choose the other example to sight read for your teacher.

1.

2.

Ensemble Piece

Before you begin this duet, tap and count the rhythm of the student part. In order for this piece to be effective, the rhythm must be steady. Keep your eyes on the music and count as you play.

Eighths are Enough

Teacher accompaniment (student plays as written)

? After playing, ask yourself, "Were all of my eighth notes steady?"

Unit 2

Review of intervals (2nds through 5ths);
melodies starting on treble G and bass F;
legato/staccato; ¾ time signature

DAY ONE

Rhythm—Clap the following rhythmic examples and whisper the counting!   **DID IT!**

Sight reading—Tap and count the rhythm before playing.
Play the examples without stopping, keeping your eyes on the music.

DAY TWO

Rhythm—Knock on the wood of the piano wherever you see an "X"
on a notehead.   **DID IT!**

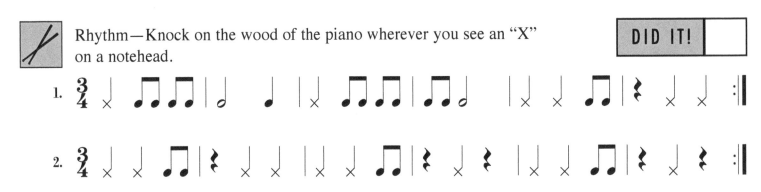

Sight reading—Count the rhythm of these melodies silently while following the music with your eyes.
Plan the sound before playing!

10

Rhythm—Speak the lyrics in rhythm while you point to each note.

DID IT!

1. Hear the crick-ets sing a-long in the eve-ning twi-light. Lis-ten to their songs.

2. One of my fav-'rite things to do is to make slim-y mud pies.

Sight reading—Before playing: tap the rhythm, then play the melodic line silently on the fallboard of the piano.

DAY FOUR

Rhythm—Add bar lines to the following rhythms.
Then tap the rhythms with your feet!

DID IT!

Sight reading—Silently play both examples on the fallboard, taking care to use the correct articulations. Then play out loud.

Rhythm—Tap the following rhythmic examples.
Count out loud with energy in your voice!

Sight reading—Silently play these melodies on the top of the keys at ♩ = 84. Keep a steady beat while you play and listen to the rise and fall of the melody. Then play without stopping.

Rhythm—Tap each line, using the right hand for the upstems and the left hand for the downstems. Then have your teacher tap the other part at the same time.

Sight reading—Find and circle all of the harmonic thirds in each example.
Then play each line without stopping.

12

FJH15

Ensemble Piece

DID IT!

Before you begin this duet, point to the notes and count the rhythm of the piece. Silently play the duet, making all of the *staccato* notes short. Keep your eyes on the music and count as you play.

The Dancing Chickens

Teacher accompaniment (student plays one octave higher than written)

? After playing, ask yourself, "Did the piece sound like its title?"

Unit 3

Review of intervals (2nds through 5ths);
melodies starting on treble C and bass C;
$\frac{2}{4}$ time signature

DAY ONE

Rhythm—Clap the following rhythmic examples and count out loud.

DID IT! ☐

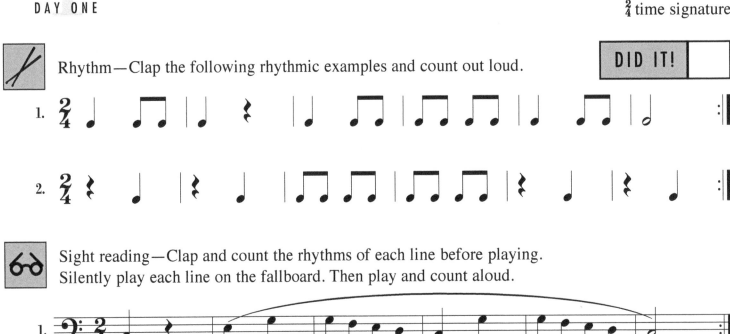

Sight reading—Clap and count the rhythms of each line before playing.
Silently play each line on the fallboard. Then play and count aloud.

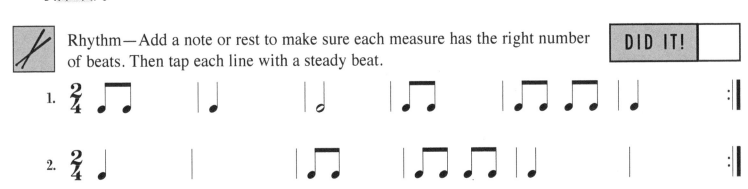

DAY TWO

Rhythm—Add a note or rest to make sure each measure has the right number
of beats. Then tap each line with a steady beat.

DID IT! ☐

Sight reading—Count the rhythm of these melodies silently while following the music with your
eyes. Then play them without stopping!

14

DAY THREE

Rhythm—Speak the lyrics in rhythm while you point to each note.

DID IT!

1. I can count in two four, Watch me count in two four, It's a piece of cake!

2. Two plus two is four. Four plus four is eight. Eight plus eight is six-teen.

Sight reading—Tap the rhythm before playing.
Counting while you play will help you keep a steady beat!

DAY FOUR

Rhythm—Add bar lines to the following rhythms. Then whisper
the rests and tap the rhythm of the notes on your lap or on the fallboard.

DID IT!

Sight reading—Silently play these examples first.
Then play each line from beginning to end without stopping.

Rhythm—Clap each example twice, first *forte* then *piano*.

DID IT!

Sight reading—With the metronome set at ♩ = 80, clap or tap each example.
Then play each at the same metronome speed. Always look ahead!

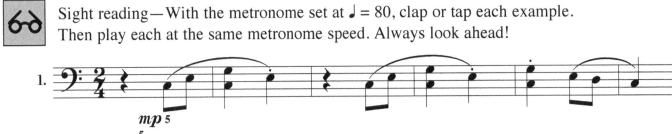

★ LESSON DAY

Rhythm—Clap and count each rhythmic line with energy and without stopping.

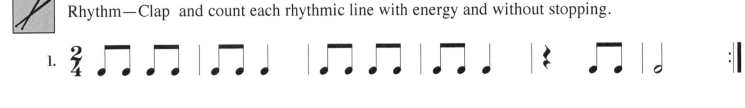

Sight reading—Circle all of the bass C's below.
Keep your eyes on the music as you play, and listen for a *legato* sound.

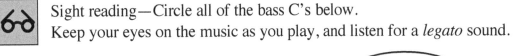

Ensemble Piece

DID IT!

Before you begin this duet, find bass C. From there, find the fourth interval. Think about playing this piece with a steady beat and with energy!

Oom Pah

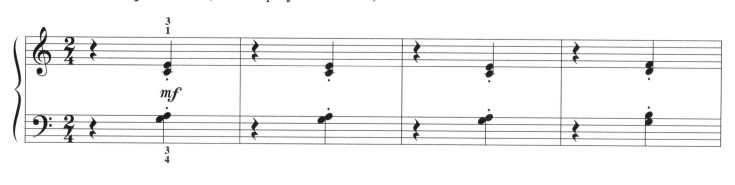

Teacher accompaniment (student plays as written)

 After playing, ask yourself, "Did we play this duet with energy and life?"

Unit 4

DAY ONE

Rhythm—Clap the following rhythmic examples and whisper the rests!

DID IT!	

DAY TWO

Rhythm—Clap or tap the following rhythms.
Accent the downbeats as you count along!

DID IT!	

Sight reading—Clap and count the melodies while following the music with your eyes.
Then play with confidence!

Key of A major

Key of E major

FJH153

Rhythm—Speak the lyrics in rhythm while you point to each note.

DID IT!

1.

Hel - lo.   Hel - lo.   How ya' do-in?   Just fine.   See ya!   Bye!

2.

Mov-ies a-bout su - per -he-roes   are   the   best.   What kind of mov-ies do   you like?

Sight reading—Tap the rhythm before playing.
Play the melody without stopping, observing all pitches and rhythms!

1.

2.

Rhythm—Add bar lines to the following rhythms.
Then, count the rhythms marching in place, if you'd like.

DID IT!

1.

2.

Sight reading—Silently play these examples on the top of the keys.
Then play at a tempo that will keep you from stopping.

1.

2.

Rhythm—Add a note or rest to complete each measure. Then clap and count.

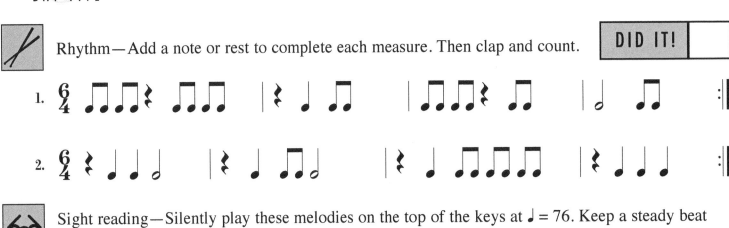

Sight reading—Silently play these melodies on the top of the keys at ♩ = 76. Keep a steady beat while you play and observe all articulations. Try playing the examples again at a faster speed!

⭐ LESSON DAY

Rhythm—Clap each rhythm slowly, then once again quickly.
You can decide with your teacher if it was steady!

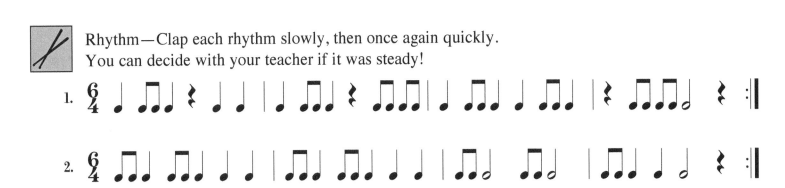

Sight reading—Circle the tonic notes in each example below.
Listen for a steady pulse as you play slowly with confidence!

Ensemble Piece

Before you begin this duet, point to the notes and count the rhythm of the piece. Circle all the harmonic thirds. Keep your eyes on the music and keep it steady as you play.

California Breeze

With warmth

Teacher accompaniment (student plays as written)

After playing, ask yourself, "Did the duet sound breezy?"

Unit 5

New Concept: minor five-finger
patterns: A, D, and E

DAY ONE

Rhythm—Clap the following rhythmic examples and count with energy!

DID IT!

Sight reading—Circle all of the harmonic thirds. Can you find one melodic third
and block it (play together)? Then play as written with a steady tempo!

Key of A minor

Key of D minor

DAY TWO

Rhythm—Tap each rhythm twice—the first time *forte*, then *piano*.

DID IT!

Sight reading—Clap and count the examples. Play with energy, observing all articulations and rests.

Key of E minor

Key of D minor

FJH153

Rhythm—Speak the lyrics in rhythm while you point to each note.

DID IT!

1.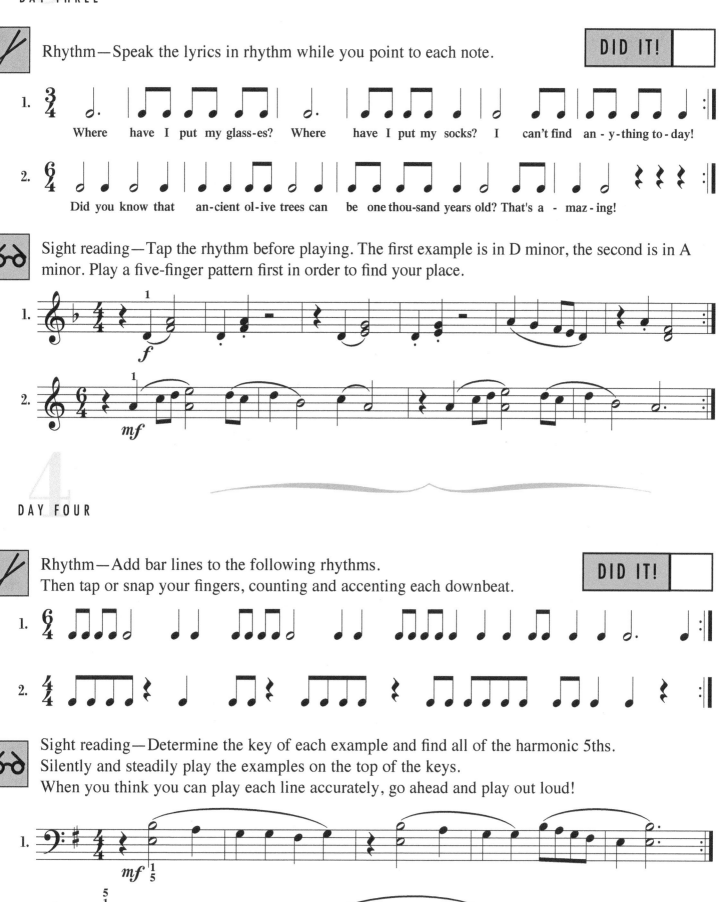

Where have I put my glass-es? Where have I put my socks? I can't find an - y-thing to - day!

2. Did you know that an-cient ol-ive trees can be one thou-sand years old? That's a - maz - ing!

Sight reading—Tap the rhythm before playing. The first example is in D minor, the second is in A minor. Play a five-finger pattern first in order to find your place.

4

DAY FOUR

Rhythm—Add bar lines to the following rhythms.
Then tap or snap your fingers, counting and accenting each downbeat.

DID IT!

Sight reading—Determine the key of each example and find all of the harmonic 5ths.
Silently and steadily play the examples on the top of the keys.
When you think you can play each line accurately, go ahead and play out loud!

Rhythm—Count out loud, whispering all of the rests in the examples below.

1.

2.

 Sight reading—With the metronome set at ♩ = 92, clap or tap the following examples.
Then play them at the same metronome speed. Repeat the process at ♩ = 104.

★ LESSON DAY

 Rhythm—Clap one of these examples for your teacher.
Could your teacher tell which example you performed? Clap the other example together.

1.

2.

 Sight reading—Determine the key of each example below.
Plan the fingering and phrasing. Then play each, listening for a steady beat.

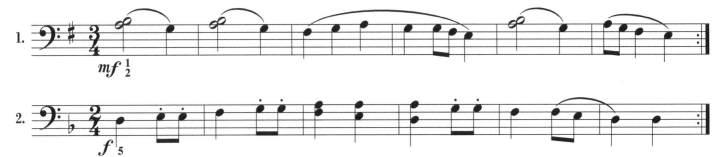

FJH15.

Ensemble Piece

DID IT!

Before you begin this duet, tap and count the rhythm of the student part. Then block (play together) all of the intervals that are circled. Finally, play the original version. Keep your eyes on the music and count as you play!

Interruptions

Teacher accompaniment (student plays as written)

? After playing, ask yourself, "Were my *staccato* notes detached?"

Unit 6

DAY ONE

Rhythm—Clap the following rhythmic examples and count with confidence!

DID IT!

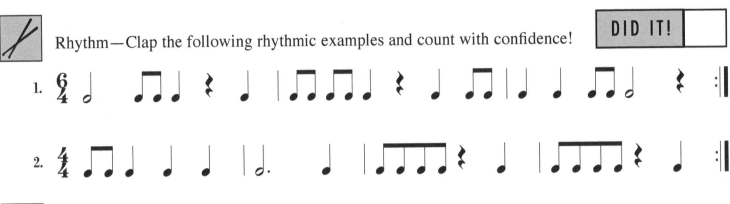

Sight reading—Plan ahead: look at the key signature, fingering, and articulations.
Clap and count the examples. Play each example twice without stopping.

DAY TWO

Rhythm—Clap or tap the following rhythms. On all of the "X" notes, snap
your fingers or knock on the wood of the piano.

DID IT!

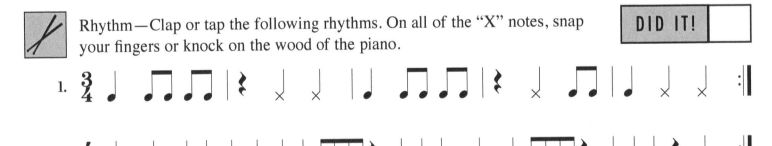

Sight reading—Prepare by planning the tempo and the key. Play with confidence and don't stop!

FJH153

Rhythm—Speak the lyrics in rhythm while you point to each note.

DID IT!

1. I have to do my home-work.　　I can't come out to - day.　　When will it be a week-end?

2. I like bugs.　　Ick - y squish-y bugs.　　On the ground, in the air,　　eve-ry - where!

Sight reading—Determine the key. Circle the tonic notes throughout each example.
Then tap the rhythm before playing. Counting while you play will help you keep the beat.

1. *mp*

2. *f*

Rhythm—Add bar lines to the following rhythms.
Then tap the rhythm on your lap, accenting each downbeat.

DID IT!

1.

2.

Sight reading—Determine the key of each example and find all of the harmonic intervals.
Silently and steadily play the examples on the top of the keys. When you think you can play each
line accurately, go ahead and play out loud!

1. *p*

2. *mp*　　*mf*

Rhythm—Tap the upstems with your right hand and the downstems with your left.

 Sight reading—With the metronome set at ♩ = 92, clap or tap the following examples. Then play these at the same metronome speed. Repeat the process at ♩ = 104.

★ LESSON DAY

 Rhythm—Your teacher will clap one of the following examples. Point to the rhythm you hear your teacher clap. Then choose the other example to clap. Can you clap either example from memory?

 Sight reading—Your teacher will play one of the following melodies. Point to the one you hear. Can you clap this rhythm from memory? Then sight read both examples.

Ensemble Piece

Before you begin this duet, clap and count the rhythm of the student part, whispering the rests. Decide if the intervals are melodic seconds, thirds, fourths, or fifths. Imagine a scene that matches the title. Keep your eyes on the music as you play.

Noises from the Attic

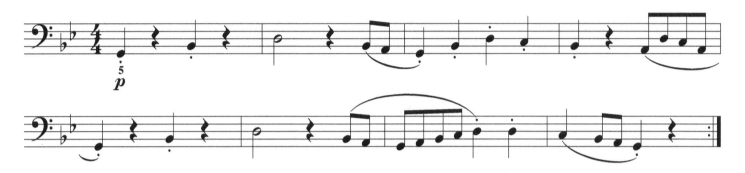

Teacher accompaniment (student plays as written)

? After playing, ask yourself, "Did this piece sound mysterious and creepy?"

Unit 7

DAY ONE

Rhythm—Clap the following rhythmic example and count. Accent the downbeats.

DID IT!

Keep going!

Sight reading—Before playing: count while pointing to each beat. Circle all of the melodic 3rds. Do you notice that the same F is shared by your two thumbs? Then play with a strong pulse.

Keep going!

DAY TWO

Rhythm—Clap the following example while you count. Follow the *crescendo* markings, too!

DID IT!

Sight reading—Circle the middle C guide notes for each hand. Feel the pulse of the rhythm as you play!

Keep going!

30

FJH15

Rhythm—Speak the lyrics in rhythm while you point to each note.

DID IT!

Keep going!

My fav-'rite time of year is when the   leaves start to change col-ors, and it   gets a lit-tle cold-er.

I love Sep-tem-ber, I love Oc-to-ber,   I love No-vem-ber!   It's my   fav-'rite time of year.

Sight reading—Tap the rhythm before playing. Plan the dynamics and phrasing before starting.

Rhythm—Add bar lines to the following rhythm.
Then tap the rhythm with your feet!

DID IT!

Sight reading—Clap and count the following example before playing.
Can you clap the rhythm of the first phrase without looking at the music?

Rhythm—Fill in the missing beats of each measure with a note or rest.
Then clap and count.

DID IT!

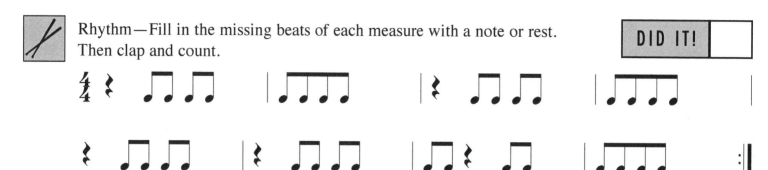

Sight reading—With the metronome set at ♩ = 96, clap or tap the following melodic line.
Then play it at the same speed. If you make a mistake, keep going!

⭐ **LESSON DAY**

Rhythm—Start clapping the following example and have your teacher start one measure after you.
Keep a steady pulse and listen to your teacher ending one measure after you!

Sight reading—Plan ahead: study the key and the rhythm.
Circle all of the guide note F's. Play with a *staccato* touch!

Ensemble Piece

DID IT!

Before you begin this duet, count the rhythm, pointing to each note. Circle the first G of the right hand and the first G of the left hand. Keep your eyes on the music and count as you play.

Tribal Dance

Teacher accompaniment (student plays as written)

? After playing, ask yourself, "Did this piece have the steady beat of a tribal dance?"

Unit 8

DAY ONE

Rhythm—Clap the following rhythmic example and count with confidence!

DID IT!

Keep going!

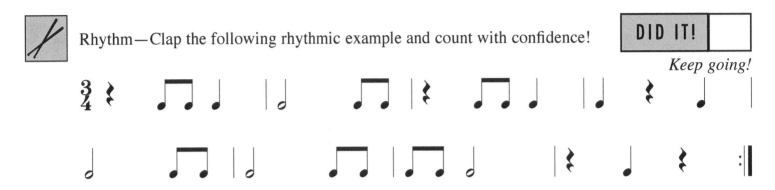

Sight reading—Tap and count the rhythm before playing. Place your thumbs on the same D.
Then play the example at a tempo that will allow you to play accurately.

DAY TWO

Rhythm—Create a melody using the A five-finger pattern from the following
rhythm. Play it with a steady pulse.

DID IT!

Sight reading—Plan before playing: clap and count.
Look at the time and key signatures. Where is the only G sharp?

FJH15

Rhythm—Speak the lyrics in rhythm while you point to each note.

DID IT!

When I was five, I learned to tie my shoes, and when I was six, I learned to ride my bike.

When I was sev-en, I start-ed the pi-an-o and now I can do al-most an-y-thing!

Sight reading—Tap the rhythm before playing.
Set a strong rhythmic pulse and play without stopping.

Rhythm—Add bar lines to the following rhythm. When you have finished, clap and count the example at the tempo of your choice.

DID IT!

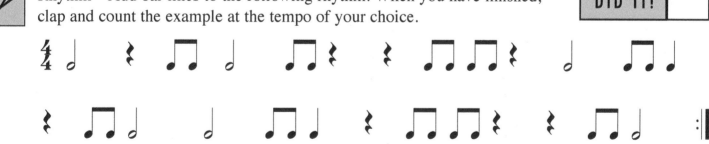

Sight reading—Plan ahead: study the rhythm and the key. Where are the 3rds? Do you see any 5ths?

Rhythm—Count silently and play the following example using the notes from a D major five-finger scale.

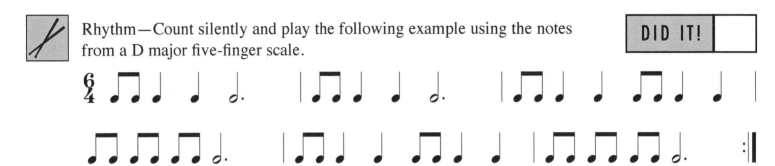

DID IT! ☐

Sight reading—With the metronome set at ♩ = 96, clap or tap the following example. Then play it at the same metronome speed. If you make a mistake, keep going!

★ LESSON DAY

Rhythm—Clap the top line while your teacher claps the bottom line. When you get to the end, switch lines without stopping!

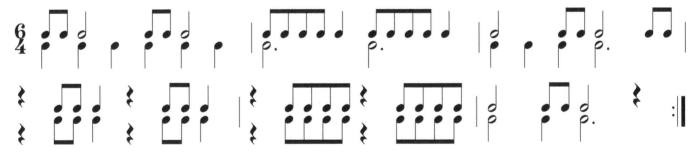

Sight reading—Circle all of the 3rds in the melody below. Then play it with a steady beat and *legato* touch!

FJH15

Ensemble Piece

DID IT!

Before you begin this duet, clap and count the rhythm of the student part. Block all of the intervals of a 4th (play them together) with a *forte* sound. Keep your eyes on the music as you play.

Marching Tubas

Teacher accompaniment (student plays one octave lower)

 After playing, ask yourself, "Was the rhythm steady like a march and were the *staccato* notes short?"

Unit 9

DAY ONE

Rhythm—Clap the following rhythmic example and count loudly. Whisper when you count a rest!

DID IT! [ ]

Sight reading—Plan ahead: look at the key and time signature. Clap and count the entire example. Then play at a slow tempo without stopping. Once you can play this example in C major, transpose it to D major (play each note one step higher than written).

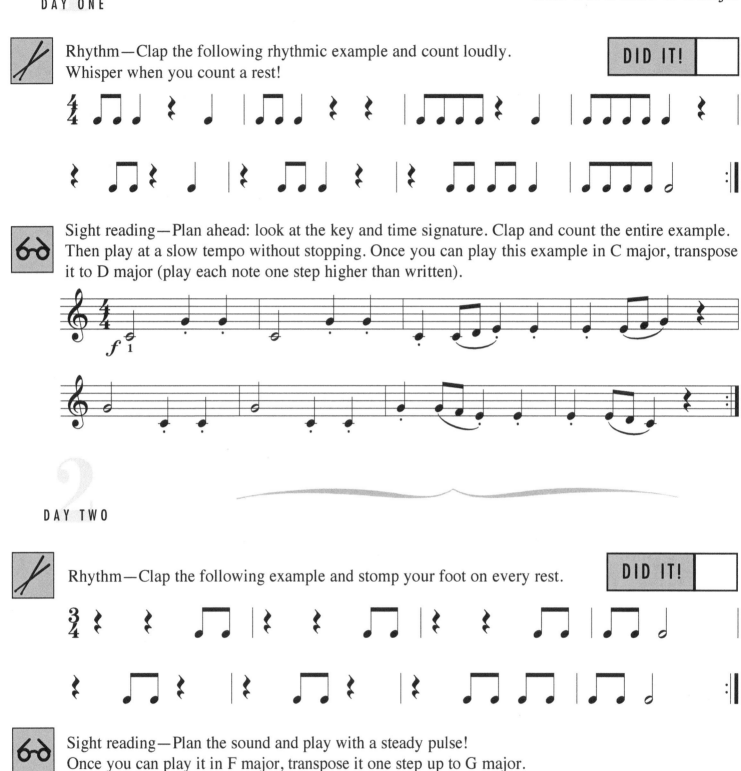

DAY TWO

Rhythm—Clap the following example and stomp your foot on every rest.

DID IT! [ ]

Sight reading—Plan the sound and play with a steady pulse!
Once you can play it in F major, transpose it one step up to G major.

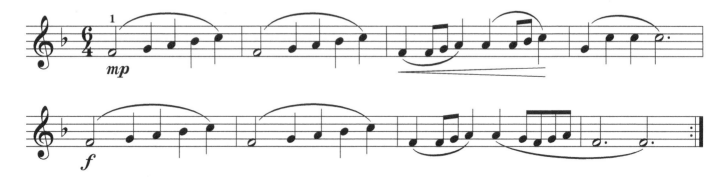

Rhythm—Speak the lyrics in rhythm while you point to each note.

DID IT! ☐

Once I had the worst dream.   I dreamt I for-got how to play the   pia-no!   When

I woke up,   I went to the   pia-no just   to   see if I could still   play!

Sight reading—Clap and count the next example. Then play it at a slow tempo without stopping. Then, transpose it one step up to D major.

DAY FOUR

Rhythm—Add bar lines to the following rhythms. When you have finished, clap and count each line twice.

DID IT! ☐

Sight reading—Slowly and silently play this example on the top of the piano keys. Then play it as written at a tempo that will keep you from stopping. Then, transpose it one step up to G major.

Rhythm—Count silently and play the following rhythm using the notes of a D major five-finger scale.

DID IT!

Sight reading—Silently play the melody on the top of the keys at ♩ = 96. Keep a steady, slow beat. Can you transpose this melody to D major?

★ LESSON DAY

Rhythm—Your teacher will start to clap this example one measure after you begin. Keep a steady beat, and listen as your teacher finishes one measure after you do.

Sight reading—Study the rhythm and play the following example from beginning to end, without stopping. Choose a tempo that will allow you to play accurately. Can you transpose this melody to G major for your teacher?

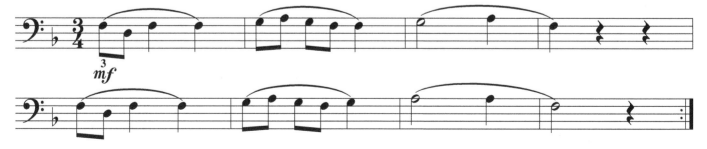

Ensemble Piece

DID IT!

Before you begin this duet, clap and count the rhythm of the student part. Then tap your part while your teacher taps the teacher part. Does the teacher part ever imitate rhythms from the student part?

Kangaroo Races

Teacher accompaniment (student plays one octave higher)

? After playing, ask yourself, "Did the piece sound like the title?"

Unit 10

Review of all concepts

DAY ONE

 Rhythm—Clap the following rhythmic example and count once *piano* and once *forte*. When you see a rest, whisper!

DID IT!

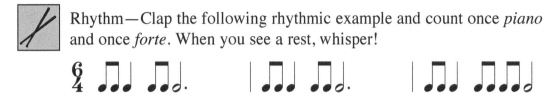

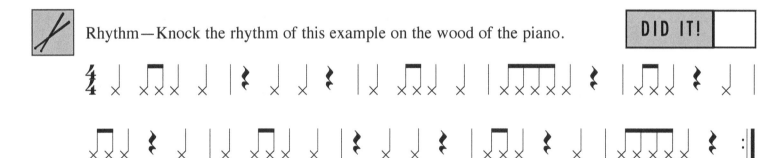 Sight reading—Tap and count the rhythm. Can you tap the first line from memory? Then play the entire melody with energy!

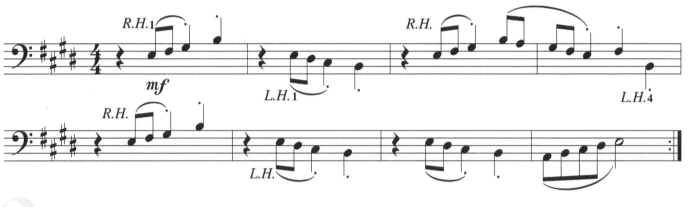

DAY TWO

 Rhythm—Knock the rhythm of this example on the wood of the piano.

DID IT!

Sight reading—Count the rhythm of this melody silently while following the music with your eyes. Notice that your second fingers play the same A.

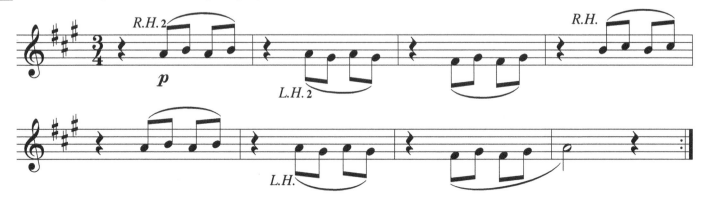

Rhythm—Speak the lyrics in rhythm while you point to each note.

Sight reading—Tap the rhythm before playing. Determine the key of this example and find the opening position of each hand before starting. Set a strong rhythmic pulse and play without stopping.

4

DAY FOUR

Rhythm—Add bar lines to the following rhythms.
When you have finished, tap the example with your feet.

Sight reading—With your hands in your lap, look at the music and think about where you will place them to begin. Then move your hands to the correct location on the keyboard.

Rhythm—Fill in the correct time signature for the example below.
Then clap the example while counting at *mezzo forte*.

DID IT!

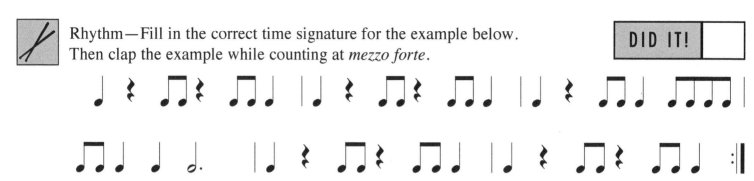

Sight reading—With the metronome set at ♩ = 100, clap or tap the following example.
Then play it at the same speed. If you make a tiny mistake, keep going.

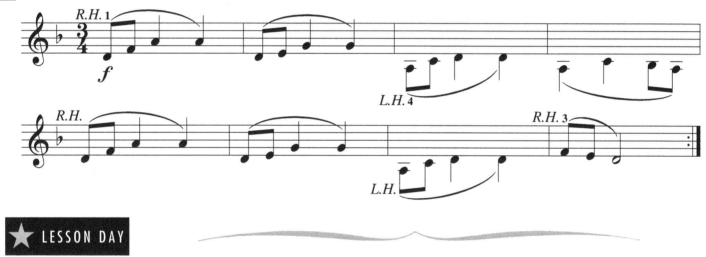

★ **LESSON DAY**

Rhythm—Your teacher will start to clap this example one measure after you begin. (This is called
a *round*). Clapping and counting steadily will make sure that you end exactly one measure apart.

Sight reading—Your teacher will play this example, making one mistake on purpose.
Point to the place you hear the mistake. Then play the example perfectly!

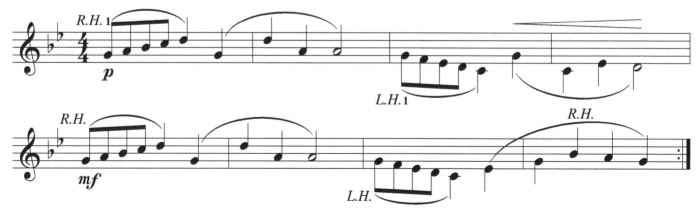

FJH153

Ensemble Piece

Before you begin this duet, silently play the piece on the fallboard. Which key do both thumbs play?

Mysterious Mansion

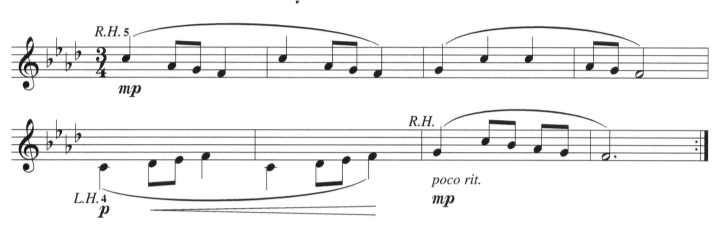

Teacher accompaniment (student plays one octave higher)

 After playing, ask yourself, "Did I follow all of the dynamic markings? Did it sound mysterious? Did I keep going no matter what?"

Sight Reading and Rhythm Review

Clap and count the following eight-measure examples out loud. Keep a steady beat, and don't stop!

DID IT!

Tap the following four-measure examples, using your right hand for the upstems and your left hand for the downstems. Keep your eyes on the music!

DID IT!

FJH15

• Play the following harmonic and melodic intervals. Then write the intervals.

Example:

harmonic 3rd   melodic 4th

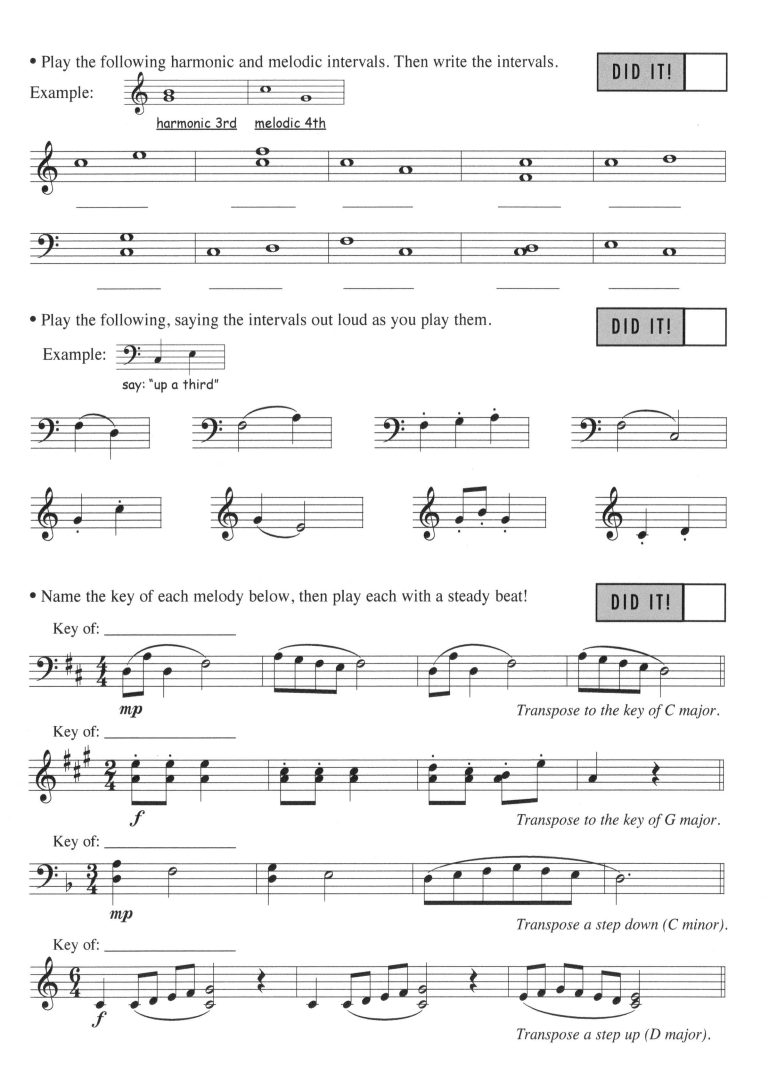

• Play the following, saying the intervals out loud as you play them.

Example:

say: "up a third"

• Name the key of each melody below, then play each with a steady beat!

Key of: _____

mp

Transpose to the key of C major.

Key of: _____

f

Transpose to the key of G major.

Key of: _____

mp

Transpose a step down (C minor).

Key of: _____

f

Transpose a step up (D major).

H1537

Additional Sight Reading Exercises

Unit 1: Clap and count out loud before playing.

Unit 2: Silently play these examples on the tops of the keys.

FJH153

8.

9.

10.

Unit 3: Clap and count the melodies while following the music with your eyes.
   Then, play with confidence!

11.

12.

13.

14.

15.

Unit 4: Listen for a steady pulse as you play.

16.

17.

18.

19.

20.

Unit 5: Play steadily and with energy!

21.

FJH15

22.

fingering? ___

23.

24.

25.

26.

Unit 6: Think through the rhythm and the notes before playing.

fingering? ___

27.

28.

29.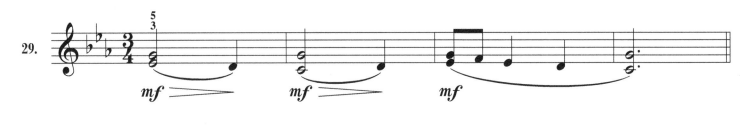

30.

fingering? ___

31.

32.

Unit 7: Plan carefully before beginning to play.

33.

34.

35.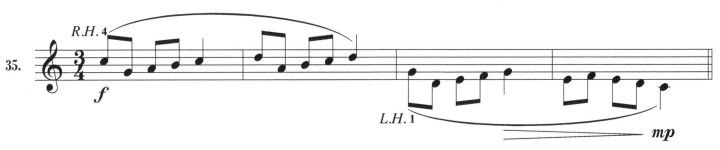

Unit 8: Tap the rhythm before playing.

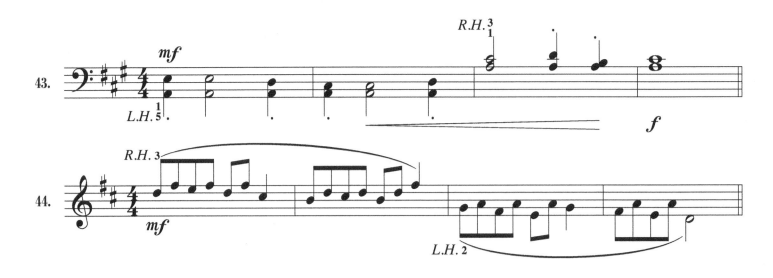

Unit 9: After playing these exercises, transpose them.

(Transpose to D Major)

(Transpose to G Major)

(Transpose to D Major)

Unit 10: Count out loud while playing. Once you start, don't stop until the end!

Certificate of Achievement

_____

has successfully completed

SIGHT READING &
RHYTHM EVERY DAY®

BOOK 2A

of The FJH Pianist's Curriculum®

You are now ready for **Book 2B**

_____

Date

_____

Teacher's Signature